Our Communities

by Donna Foley

PEARSON

Scott
Foresman

Editorial Offices: Glenview, Illinois • Parsippany, New Jersey • New York, New York
Sales Offices: Needham, Massachusetts • Duluth, Georgia • Glenview, Illinois
Coppell, Texas • Sacramento, California • Mesa, Arizona

Everybody lives in a **community**. Communities are made up of neighborhoods.

An **urban** community is in a city.

A suburban community is near a city.

A **rural** community has a lot of nature.

There are many houses in a **suburb**.
The houses usually have yards.

In an urban community, neighborhoods have many buildings.
People can shop near their homes.

A rural community might have many farms.

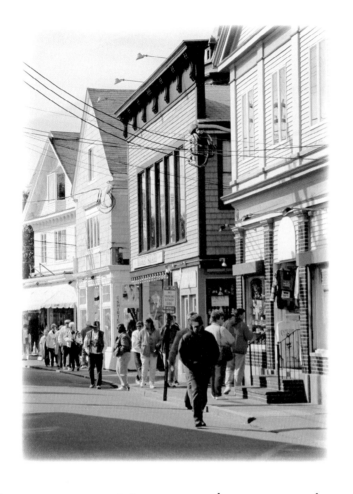

Our communities are close together.
Our communities are spread out.
Each community is special!

Glossary

community a place that is made up of many neighborhoods

rural an area with small communities and open space

suburb a type of community that is near a city

urban an area that has a city